IF PIGS COULD TALK

The Case for a Plant-Based Diet

ROGER GLOSS

Roger Gloss
30 May 17

This book is dedicated to those who embraced this broader definition of environmental justice and compassion long before I had any idea. You have transformed and enriched my life.

I have battled this corporate leviathan for more than a decade through public lectures and in books. ... I had thought I understood most of the inner workings of corporate power. But I was mistaken. There was one huge hole I had missed.

Chris Hedges

Contents

INTRODUCTION

This book is a short course on the destructive impacts of animal agriculture upon our planet and the importance for humanity to convert to a plant-based diet. Many excellent books have been written on this subject, most of them in fairly recent times. At the end of this book I will recommend some of them for further reading. I am far from an authority on this subject; it is only recently that I've learned anything at all about it. But my education came unexpectedly and quickly. It was an intensely personal journey in which I was forced to examine my core values and make some fundamental adjustments to my behavior.

My purpose in writing this book is to share my journey with you, and to do this as concisely and as convincingly as possible. I was helped along the way by friends, documentaries, books, nonprofit organizations, and other resources. I wish, though, that there had been some single, compact resource – a handbook of sorts – that could have brought me sooner to where I am, with fewer detours and missteps along the way. My hope is that this book will prove to be such a resource for you.

I've drawn on the experience, writings, and prior research of experts on the subject of animal agriculture. I've done my best to represent their findings and data accurately. In the end, though, any errors or inaccuracies in this short book – hopefully minor – are my own.

In my view, the evidence is compelling that we need to stop consuming animal products. The time for transformation is now.

ONE

Numbers

70 billion

Land animals raised and killed for food each year, globally. That's 10 animals for every one of the 7 billion people on the planet. However, the United States consumes a far greater share of the world's meat – see below – while many people in the third world consume *none*.

9 billion

Land animals slaughtered each year in the United States. There are 320 million people in the United States. Although some meat is exported, that's one eighth of the world's animals slaughtered by or for roughly one twentieth of the world's population.

Let me break this down a little further, to make it more personal:
- 28.8 million cattle
- 115.4 million hogs
- 8.8 *billion* chickens, ducks, and turkeys
- 2.3 million sheep and lambs

970 – 2,700 billion

Fishes caught from the wild each year, globally. (This estimate is calculated using reported tonnages and mean weights of the various fish species.) To these mind-boggling numbers, we need to add farm-raised seafood:

- 37 – 120 billion farmed fish
- 21 – 40 billion crayfish, crabs, and lobsters
- 150 – 380 billion shrimps and prawns

86 times

Potency of methane as a greenhouse gas in the atmosphere, compared to carbon dioxide (from fossil fuels). Methane is a major byproduct of raising livestock. In various sources I have seen this multiplier ranging from 25 to 100, depending on the methodology used to assess Global Warming Potential (GWP). The point is that, clearly, methane in our atmosphere is far more damaging than carbon dioxide.

18%

Percent of greenhouse gas emissions each year, globally, from livestock production. Compare this to 13 percent from the entire transportation sector.

660

Gallons of water required to produce one hamburger. This is roughly equivalent to two months of taking showers.

70%

Percent of all water consumption in the eleven western states that is used to raise animals for food.

99%

Percent of all farmed animals in the United States raised on factory farms, where treatment of animals is least humane.

222

Pounds of meat and seafood consumed per person per year in the United States. This is comprised of:
- 58 pounds of beef
- 46 pounds of pork
- 102 pounds of poultry
- 16 pounds of fish and shellfish

16

Pounds of grain fed to cattle to produce one pound of beef.

349 pounds

Your weight at age 2 if you grew as fast as a factory-farmed chicken.

TWO

Behind the Numbers

Numbers tell a powerful story. When describing a situation or problem, numbers help us understand its magnitude. They *quantify*. In today's complex society where we have to make trade-offs – because we simply can't deal with all challenges at once – numbers help to answer questions like, how big is it? How harmful is it? Is Thing 1 larger or smaller than Thing 2? Is Problem A or Problem B more urgent?

Numbers can also be confusing. They can be controversial, debatable, sometimes even misleading or deceptive. In order to best fend off challenges to their validity, numbers must be put into a specific context and thoroughly explained and defended. For a topic as controversial and polarizing as animal agriculture (or climate change), a single inaccuracy, exaggeration, or flaw in the data might be subject to vicious attack, exploited by powerful forces of the status quo to discredit the entire argument.

In my own view, the numbers in the previous chapter are fairly straightforward and very powerful. I've sourced them carefully, primarily from the books under "Recommended Reading and Viewing" at the end of this book. I've put these numbers out there to grab your attention, to inform you and, yes, to perhaps shock and surprise you.

For data junkies like me, numbers alone might suffice to affect my behavior and beliefs. But numbers tell only part of the story. The rest follows here.

There are a number of compelling reasons why humanity should convert to a plant-based diet. As with most transformations, these reasons are based upon the benefits of doing so, weighed against the adverse effects of *not* doing so. Because of the sheer magnitude of the animal agriculture industry in the United States as well as globally, it's fair to say that the gulf between continuing our present habits and making the transition to a plant-based diet is the difference between continuing to degrade global climate and environment and building a more sustainable, equitable existence for everyone on the planet.

If you're thinking right now that this sounds grandiose, I hope you can hold back your skepticism until you've read further. The next few chapters explore vital aspects of our lives, our environment, and our very future that are impacted adversely by animal agriculture:

- Climate – The effect on global climate of greenhouse gas emissions (GHG) from animal agriculture
- Land – Competition for land resources; depletion and degradation of land
- Water – Wasteful use of increasingly scarce water reserves; pollution of drinking water and runoff
- Animal treatment
- Pollution – Of air, water, and land
- Labor – The toll of factory farm jobs on workers who perform them

- Health – The effects on human health of meat and dairy consumption
- Sustainability – Dealing with the question of whether we can continue current industry practices

The devil, of course, is in the details within each of the following chapters.

THREE

Climate

I consider myself an environmentalist. Since the 1970s I've believed that global population growth is placing unbearable strain on our air, water, and natural resources. Despite being part of the typical American high-consumption lifestyle, I've kept a mindset of doing countless little things to reduce my environmental footprint: driving fuel-efficient cars; recycling; using public transportation when possible; minimizing food waste (and waste in general); conserving water; avoiding disposable plastic like the plague; getting as much useful life as possible out of my cars, computers and other possessions; and generally trying to *buy less stuff*.

Then, in the new century, along came Al Gore and his 2006 documentary *An Inconvenient Truth*. Add climate change to my longtime concern for the environment. Although I might have been slow to learn about it, once I knew the facts – and, please, let's not waste time here debating the science – I became a passionate believer.

The burning of fossil fuels since the dawn of the Industrial Revolution is spewing carbon dioxide into the atmosphere at an alarming rate, which in turn is increasing average global temperatures, melting polar ice, causing sea levels to rise, and precipitating wildfires, droughts, and other extreme weather events. Imbalances in our atmosphere caused by burning fossil fuels upset balances in our oceans that are critical to a stable climate, and vice versa. Feedback loops between our oceans and atmosphere have the potential to make the planet unlivable much sooner than scientists originally thought. We are playing a dangerous game.

But what to do? Fossil fuels are the problem, right? Our entire consumer-driven economy has been built on a foundation of fossil fuels, whether we strip them off mountaintops in the Appalachians, import them from nasty countries in the Middle East, drill for them offshore, extract them from tar sands, or frack them with dangerous chemicals from rock deep underground.

Weaning ourselves from fossil fuels is a daunting task, even more so as the oil and gas industry resists every step of the way.

We feel pretty helpless. Increasingly, there are choices we can make, as individuals, to help fight climate change: electric cars, solar roofs, energy efficient appliances and light bulbs. Sometimes, though, there is a short-term cost to these choices that is beyond the means of many of us. And making measurable progress in this way, solely through individual actions, is painfully slow.

The Paris climate accord signed by 195 nations in 2015 was truly a breakthrough. Although its goals are not aggressive enough and the commitments by signatory nations are non-binding, it nevertheless demonstrates that the vast majority of nations accounting for the vast majority of global greenhouse gas emissions (GHG) now clearly recognize the realities of climate change and the need to act.

Ultimately, strong federal action will be necessary here in the United States, the world's second largest source of greenhouse gases (only recently surpassed by China) to meet our commitments under the Paris accord.

When will this happen? It's hard to imagine it happening at all in today's toxic political environment, where the boundary between corporate capitalism and government is fuzzy indeed, and the U.S. Congress is peppered with supposed climate deniers.

Then, another decade later, along came Kip Andersen and his 2014 documentary *Cowspiracy: The Sustainability Secret.* If Al Gore triggered my first climate change epiphany, Kip Andersen bears responsibility for my second. As the film's subtitle implies, there is a secret regarding climate change that has been carefully kept from us by the animal agriculture industry, by its protectors in federal government, and – as documented in the film – with even environmental organizations such as the Sierra Club and Greenpeace complicit. The great Al Gore himself avoided the topic of animal agriculture. He felt that he already had a big enough fight on his hands against the fossil fuel industry.

But here is the reality. Animal agriculture is responsible for more greenhouse gas emissions globally than the entire transportation sector. This is because methane, a major byproduct of factory farming, is nearly a hundred times more potent in the atmosphere than carbon dioxide. Nitrous oxide, a byproduct of production of petrochemical fertilizers, used to grow feed grains for livestock, is even more potent than methane.

And while we're at it, there are other destructive greenhouse gas effects of animal agriculture as well. Plenty of carbon dioxide is emitted in growing soy and corn as feed for cattle and pigs and then transporting it to factory farms. Still more carbon dioxide is emitted transporting farm animals to centralized feedlots and slaughterhouses and then transporting the resulting meat products to distant markets.   Land for raising cattle is the major reason for clearing the Amazon rainforest at alarming rates.   This is a double-whammy to climate, because burning trees releases stored carbon dioxide *into* the atmosphere, and fewer trees mean less absorption of carbon dioxide *from* the atmosphere.

Howard Lyman is a former Montana cattle rancher in his late sixties who no longer raises – or eats – meat.   His epiphany occurred long before mine.   He also possesses a compelling presence such that when he talks, people listen.   At the end of *Cowspiracy*, Howard Lyman looked me in the eye and said, "If you eat meat, don't call yourself an environmentalist."

Thus began my transformation to a vegan, i.e., plant-based, diet.

FOUR

Land

Raising animals for meat represents a miserably inefficient use of land, besides having destructive effects on the land that is used.

First let's take a conceptual look at land use, and let's focus on cattle. Cattle in the United States are either grain-fed or grass-fed. Grain-fed cattle live in confined environments or CAFOs (Concentrated Animal Feeding Operations) and are fed mostly corn, which is not their natural diet. The corn is grown elsewhere and then transported. Grass-fed cattle live in more spacious surroundings and feed on a more natural diet which grows right under their feet.

Now consider this. It takes 16 pounds of grain to produce one pound of beef (grain-fed). Meanwhile, a billion people in the world go to sleep hungry at night. What if we fed those 16 pounds of grain to people instead of feeding it to cattle (so that we, the most overfed people on earth, can eat one pound of beef)? To extrapolate further, world population today is 7 billion, many of whom are malnourished or starving. World population is projected to grow to 10 or 11 billion by the year 2050, although I certainly hope it won't. But if everyone switched to a plant-based diet, it would be possible to feed that entire future population of 11 billion, and then some.

But back to the present. There is a disturbing trend, motivated in part by an increasing public awareness of the poor treatment of animals on factory farms (the subject of a future chapter), toward "grass-fed" beef. This conjures visions of happy cows frolicking through green pastures and subsisting on their natural diet; it allows us, we think, to feel a little better about the beef we eat.

But here is the reality. Today nearly half of all land in the United States is already used for animal agriculture. Picture all of the contiguous United States west of a straight line running from the Dakotas south through west Texas. If Americans were to continue consuming more than 200 pounds of meat per person per year – as we currently do – and switch to entirely grass-fed, 3.7 billion acres of grazing land would be required. Unfortunately, the entire U.S. comprises only 1.9 billion acres. So all land from northern Canada, through the entire U.S., Central America, and pretty much half of South America, would become grazing land for farm animals. This would have to include mountain ranges, cities, forests, waterways, and deserts – *all* of the land.

And that's just to feed Americans.

The federal government subsidizes animal agriculture, much as it does the oil and gas industry. One way it does this is by the Bureau of Land Management (BLM) leasing land to cattle ranchers for grazing. BLM attempts to "manage" public lands by allocating the amount available for grazing each year based on specific conditions at the time, but the process clearly favors animal agriculture. Land is leased at bargain rates, even though this practice has destructive effects on native vegetation and wildlife and causes soil erosion, flooding, and water pollution.

One particularly tragic consequence of the grazing of cattle on public lands is the strain placed on the wild mustang (horse) population. In order to accommodate cattle ranchers, wild mustangs have been increasingly rounded up from federal lands and placed in confinement. These animals are made available for "adoption," but the supply far exceeds the demand. As a result, the federal government has publicly considered euthanizing the excess mustang population.

The "cattle versus horse" issue is quite complex, and it results in large part from humans having mucked with the natural environmental balance in the first place. But now that the damage has been done, we keep exacerbating the problem by making public lands available for raising cattle when we really don't have to. The costs of doing this are hidden, not factored into the price of beef, and thus end up being borne by every American, not just cattle ranchers or consumers of beef.

This argument, though, holds no water with Cliven Bundy, the Nevada cattle rancher who in 2014 led an armed standoff against federal officials because he didn't feel he should have to pay grazing fees for land adjacent to his ranch that, in his view, shouldn't belong to the government in the first place. The subsequent occupation in January 2016 by Bundy's sons and other armed militia at Malheur National Wildlife Refuge in eastern Oregon was merely a continuation of their father's stance against the very concept of public lands or "commons."

Perhaps a much better way to handle constraints on our nation's land resources would be for Americans not to eat meat.

FIVE

Water

When it comes to water, at the highest level, Howard Lyman puts it this way: "The meat industry is draining this country dry."

To break that statement down a little, I need to throw out some more numbers.

- In the U.S., 55 percent of water usage is for animal agriculture.
- In the eleven western states, 70 percent of water usage is for animal agriculture.
- In Montana, *97.5 percent* of water usage is for animal agriculture.
- In California, 47 percent of water usage is for animal agriculture.
- Worldwide, 20 to 33 percent of water usage is for animal agriculture. (Remember, we Americans are the biggest consumers of animal products.)

You get the idea. These figures include drinking water for animals, water needed to process them (such as hosing down slaughterhouses and equipment, filling scalding tanks, etc.), and water used indirectly to grow the grains that are fed to them.

Let's take a closer look at California, which is currently in the sixth year of a record drought. While residents have been under mandatory water restrictions, and have done a good job coming together to meet the drought crisis – removing turf lawns, installing drought tolerant landscaping with water-efficient sprinkler systems and smart timers, buying low-flow toilets and efficient washers – 80 percent of the state's water use is for irrigating crops. More than half of those crops are fed to animals raised for meat and dairy production (that's where the 47 percent figure above comes from).

Much ado is made in California and throughout the U.S. about the practice of hydraulic fracturing ("fracking") to obtain natural gas deeply imbedded in underground rock. I totally agree this is a problem, for a number of climate-related reasons, and because it is part of our fossil fuel addiction. Fracking does require enormous amounts of water, but, to put it in perspective, 70 to 140 *billion* gallons of water are used annually in this country for fracking, while 34 *trillion* gallons of water per year are used for animal agriculture. (Methane emissions from both industries are approximately equal, so both are disastrous for climate.)

One of the largest underground sources of water in the entire world is the Ogallala Aquifer, which runs down the entire center of the United States. The Ogallala has been around for at least three million years, but due in large part to crop irrigation, it is currently dropping at a rate of 3 to 10 feet every year. At this rate, the Ogallala will be mostly exhausted well within this century.

To bring things back to a personal level, remember that it takes 660 gallons of water to produce one hamburger; in comparison, it takes 60-120 gallons to produce one egg. The average American consumes 206 pounds of meat per year (from land animals), and more than 800 pounds of dairy and eggs. This level of consumption of animal products adds up to 405,000 gallons of water per person per year.

Meanwhile, with the depletion of the Ogallala Aquifer, the Great Lakes contain 84 percent of the surface freshwater in the U.S. (21 percent of the worldwide supply). Back in the 1980s, rather than managing our national water supply by conserving and using it in smarter ways, it was proposed that a pipeline be built to move water from the Great Lakes to the Midwest and the southwestern U.S. Fortunately such proposals were rejected.

Just as for land, which we examined in the previous chapter, there is a much better way to reduce our nation's water usage to more sustainable levels: stop eating meat.

SIX

Animal Treatment

Listening to Howard Lyman as he looked me in the eye at the end of *Cowspiracy* did a number on me. How could I consider myself an environmentalist and a climate activist and still eat meat? My concerns about climate change alone were enough to turn me toward a plant-based diet.

So here's a thought. Maybe if we all just reduce our consumption of meat and other animal products (we'll look at dairy and eggs later in this chapter) by, say, 80 percent or so, we can save the planet from environmental and climate destruction. That would be something like leaving 80 percent of known fossil fuel reserves in the ground, which is what climate experts have said we must do to limit global temperature increase (already baked in) to "acceptable" levels.

But there's still a problem. Another memorable scene in *Cowspiracy* shows, in graphic detail, the relatively "humane" slaughter of two ducks by a local farmer. I forced myself to watch this – several times. Some people just can't handle it and cover their eyes. It really doesn't matter whether you watch it or not. Most people, when confronted with the reality of an animal being slaughtered, are repelled.

There are several relevant points here. First, with industrialization and corporatization of farming over the past half century or so, most Americans today are completely disconnected from the food they eat. Meat comes in pleasing colors, sliced, diced, and neatly packaged in cellophane and polystyrene and attractively displayed in the refrigerator cases at our local supermarkets. We have no idea how it was raised, where it came from (we know country of origin if we're lucky), or what resources were consumed in bringing it to us.

Second, the factory farming industry likes things this way. Meat producers go to great lengths to keep the public from seeing what actually occurs on factory farms. In some states it is even illegal to photograph a factory farm operation from outside the property. At the same time these companies hide the unpleasant details of their operations from us, they do their best, through advertising, to pump up demand for meat and dairy products. They perpetuate misconceptions about the health benefits of eating meat and the superiority of animal protein.

The bottom line is that before you can eat meat an animal must be killed, i.e., slaughtered. Could you kill your own meat, day in and day out, if that were the only way you could eat meat? I couldn't, unless I was starving and there was no other acceptable nutrition available. But the point is we don't have to kill animals to eat, because there are perfectly good alternatives – plants – available to us. As we'll see in a later chapter, plants are not only perfectly good alternatives to meat; in many respects they're superior.

The subject of animal treatment on factory farms is an uncomfortable one, when we dare to look at it. Factory farm animals – cows, pigs, sheep, chickens, turkeys, even farm-raised fish – not only suffer horrible deaths at the hands of we humans who consider ourselves their masters, they lead short, miserable lives as well. I've seen videos and documentaries on the raising and slaughter of farm animals that, I'm confident, would horrify anyone who has made the commitment to read this far.

I'll spare you the worst. This is a book, not a film. I've refrained from including disturbing photos which, due to industry secrecy, are hard to come by in any case. I don't wish to gross anyone out, but I do feel it's important to describe key aspects of how animals are treated on industrial-scale factory farms and in the slaughterhouse. You're free to skip the remainder of this chapter, of course, but I hope you won't.

Beef

In the interest of production and profit, factory farmed cattle are generally slaughtered at an age of 14 to 16 months. (Back in the old days of local farming, a cow was typically slaughtered at 4 or 5 years of age, after living a more or less normal life grazing in open pastures.) To grow beef cattle to a full weight of 1200 pounds this quickly – truly this is "fast food" – they are stuffed with grain (mostly corn), supplemented by additional protein, drugs, and growth hormones.

Calves spend their early days in pastures, but are usually separated from their mothers long before natural weaning would occur. This is stressful for both mother and calf. The calves, partly from the stress of separation and partly from the change in diet from grass to grain, are prone to sickness. But the objective of the factory farm is to bring an animal to slaughter weight as quickly and cheaply as possible. Corn meets this need; it is cheap, especially with the help of federal subsidies. Corn is not a cow's natural diet and causes digestive and other health problems; hence the daily use of antibiotics. It is thought that by the time cattle are slaughtered at the age of 14 to 16 months, their digestive systems are pretty much played out and can't take much more. In fact, 13 percent of feedlot cattle have abscessed livers by the time they are slaughtered. They are obese, they are often not healthy, and their lives at the feedlot have been miserable.

The next – and last – step is the slaughterhouse. About three dozen cattle are loaded onto a trailer for a stressful trip to the slaughterhouse. Some don't even survive the trip. Once there they are funneled into a single-file chute that traverses a series of ramps. These chutes and ramps have been carefully designed by Temple Grandin, a professor of animal science, to minimize stress on the animal. The welfare of the animal isn't the point, though; what matters to the industry is that meat from a stressed animal is not as valuable as meat from one that is more "comfortable" with this final journey.

In brief, the single-file chute leads through a series of turns to a metal bar that lifts the animal off its feet over a declining ramp and deposits it on a conveyor belt. At the end of the conveyor belt a worker whose job title is "stunner" fires a 7-inch metal bolt into the forehead of the animal. If done correctly, the animal will be killed with the first shot. After stunning, a worker wraps a chain around the animal's foot and hooks it to an overhead trolley, which lifts the entire 1200-pound beast into the air and carries it to the bleeding area.

Here we have McDonald's to thank for this "humane" slaughter. McDonald's began auditing slaughterhouses in 1999 after reported cases of cattle being skinned while still alive. The standard to pass a McDonald's audit is for cattle to be rendered "insensible" by the first shot from the stunner 95 percent of the time. If not, a second shot is permitted. In a typical U.S. slaughterhouse, animals are slaughtered at a rate of nearly 400 per hour; one can imagine that mistakes happen. Just in case, there is another hand stunner in the bleed area, where the suspended animal's throat is cut.

I wish I didn't have to tell you this, but this is the sad truth of cattle slaughter. Small wonder that the beef industry does its best to keep these unpleasant details from the consumer.

Pork

Smithfield Foods kills about one of every four pigs each year in the United States, so we can look to the company for the "standards" of pig treatment and slaughter. Later we'll also look at pollution from Smithfield's sprawling hog operations in North Carolina.

Hundreds or even thousands of pigs are raised inside huge barns, on hard floors, with no straw or earth for cushion. There is no sunlight or fresh air. Forty 250-pound adult hogs might be kept in a single pen the size of a small apartment. In such close quarters pigs with minor wounds are at risk of cannibalism.

Temperatures soar inside the warehouses, and the air reeks of chemicals and gases from excrement. The industry manages this unpleasantness by running huge exhaust fans twenty-four/seven. If these fans break down for any reason (like power failure) pigs start dying.

Breeding sows are impregnated at seven months of age and kept in 2-by-7-foot gestation crates. These crates are so small that the sows cannot walk or turn around. Prevented from engaging in normal physical behavior, they develop skin wounds and crippling leg disorders, and their muscles atrophy. They are then moved to similarly cramped farrowing crates, where they give birth and nurse their piglets for up to three weeks. Under these conditions, more than 10 percent of piglets die before weaning. About a week after weaning, a sow is returned to the gestation crate and re-impregnated by artificial insemination.

To prevent possible spread of disease, pigs are sprayed regularly with insecticides and given a host of antibiotics. Aggression among pigs is common in close confinement; to mitigate this, tails of piglets are cut off, without painkillers. Ears are notched for identification, and males are castrated, all without painkillers. It's all about maximizing production and profit.

Slats in the hard concrete floor allow excrement to fall into catchment pits. Once enough excrement accumulates, pipes are opened, releasing excrement and any other foreign objects that may have fallen through the slats (such as insecticide bottles, stillborn pigs, or piglets accidentally crushed by their mothers) into large holding ponds, euphemistically called "lagoons" by the industry. As a side note, there have been cases where workers have fallen into these holding ponds; the ponds are so toxic that the workers have died.

You might think by now that this typical life of a Smithfield pig makes a cattle feedlot look like a health resort. The only good news for slaughter pigs is that their miserable lives are short. Because of how and what they are fed, pigs reach slaughter weight at about six months of age. I'll spare you the trip through the slaughterhouse; it's fair to assume that pigs undergo an experience there similar to that of cattle.

Not all that long ago, when I still ate meat, pork was my personal favorite. In particular, there was a local taco stand that featured on their menu a chunky pork and green chile burrito; this was an all-meat burrito containing nothing but chunks of pork simmered for hours in a savory green chile sauce. The meat was lean and tender and practically melted in your mouth, and the spicy chile masked any lingering taste of animal fat. Since then I've learned how pigs are raised, and I've seen the unpleasant details of their slaughter. I've also been up close with pigs at Farm Sanctuary, the national farm animal rescue organization co-founded by Gene Baur. And I've learned that pigs are quite possibly more intelligent than my dog, who I think is pretty smart and happens to be my best friend. Once I awakened to the realization that the meat I liked best came from the farm animal I like best, what choice did I have?

Poultry

From the standpoint of greenhouse gas emissions, land use, and impact to the environment, beef and pork production are far more damaging than poultry. So the fast food chain Chick-fil-A offers a partial solution. You've probably seen roadside billboards depicting a cow standing precariously on a ladder and painting the words "Eet more chikin" on a sign. The cow is no doubt thinking primarily of its own survival, but environmentalists and even climate activists might be tempted to take the cow's advice as a way to mitigate damage to the planet.

But remember, we've been talking about animal treatment and slaughter. By eating less beef and more chicken we merely find ourselves complicit in the slaughter of many more animals, because each life taken yields far less meat. And as we shall see, factory farm chickens and turkeys are treated no better than cows and pigs – in fact, far worse.

A "grow house" accommodates 20,000 chickens or 10,000 turkeys. This gives each chicken about half a square foot of living space, each turkey less than three square feet. To prevent aggressive pecking in such close confinement, chickens and turkeys are de-beaked. Turkeys, in addition, have their claws and snoods removed, without anesthesia.

To maximize profit, chickens and turkeys are brought to slaughter weight as quickly as possible: chickens in 42 days and turkeys in as little as 14 weeks. They suffer from joint disorders and skeletal deformities because their legs do not grow fast enough to support their heavy bodies.

Turkeys have been selectively bred to enlarge the breast. Their abnormal physique renders them incapable of mating. A few days before Thanksgiving in 2016 the *Los Angeles Times* published an op-ed, "Consider the turkey on your table," by Peter Singer, professor of bioethics at Princeton University. Besides describing the cruel conditions under which turkeys are raised, Singer recounts, in graphic detail, how factory farm turkeys are inseminated. One worker holds the male turkey upside down by its legs while a second worker masturbates it and captures the semen with a syringe. Semen is collected from males and diluted with an "extender" until the syringe is full. It is then taken to the hen house. By a gruesome process called "breaking," the hen is held feet down and the rump and tail feathers are pulled upward, forcing her vent open until the oviduct is exposed. A shot of compressed air blows the semen solution through a straw and into the oviduct. A worker is supposed to break one hen every 12 seconds, for ten hours a day. This is not the best job on which to build a career.

Singer's op-ed was more than enough for me. My main course this past Thanksgiving was a veggie burger.

The federal Humane Slaughter Act, originally passed in 1958, requires an animal to be rendered unconscious before it is slaughtered. We have seen already that enforcement for cattle is something less than 100 percent. Worse yet, though, poultry are specifically exempted from the law. So here is how birds are slaughtered. Shackled by their feet on a moving rail, they are first dipped head-first in an electrified bath, which paralyzes the muscles but isn't sufficient to numb them to pain or fear. The purpose of the bath is merely to render them motionless as they pass through a machine with a metal blade which slashes their throats. We might safely assume that this works *most* of the time. Dead or not, they are then submerged in a scalding tank to facilitate removal of their feathers. The industry has a cute name for birds who escape the blade and enter the scalding tank alive: "redskins."

Now that we know this, do we really want to "eet more chikin?"

What about Dairy and Eggs?

Okay, with inhumane treatment of farm animals in mind, then, maybe we shouldn't eat meat. But at least there's dairy – milk, butter, cheese – and eggs. At least we can get our animal protein that way, can't we? Milk and eggs are the natural output of farm animals, and no animal has to be mistreated or killed to obtain these products for human consumption, right?

Not exactly. This was never entirely true, and it isn't even remotely true in the modern era of factory farming. I'm aware that I've assaulted your sense of compassion and kindness repeatedly in the preceding pages, but unfortunately, high-volume dairy and egg production are no better than meat – and in some ways even worse.

Milk

Widespread consumption of cows' milk as a staple of human diet is only about two centuries old. Now, in the twenty-first century, medical consensus has long been that drinking milk is indispensable for children and healthful for everyone else. The dairy industry has piled on to this notion, satisfying as well as fueling consumer demand by "scientifically" breeding cows such that milk production per cow has quadrupled since 1925. High production has also been driven by pricing problems that make dairy farming profitable only with high volume, as well as federal price guarantees.

Several things are done to obtain this high volume. First, cows are artificially inseminated once a year and separated from their calves almost immediately after giving birth (which, as we have seen, is very stressful for both mother and calf). Milking continues for about ten months; after two months of milking, the cow is re-impregnated. This intensive cycle continues for three to five years, until the cow's overall milk production declines. At that point it is usually sent to slaughter.

The natural lifespan of a cow is about twenty years.

A second fundamental means to increase milk output per cow is through diet. Dairy cows are fed unnatural diets, mainly corn and soybeans, sometimes augmented by injections of bovine growth hormone (BGH). While this diet increases milk output, it also has devastating health effects on the animals; simply put, it makes them sick. Dairy operations thus walk a fine line between achieving high production and triggering serious illnesses. These include mastitis, a painful inflammation of the udder; ruminal acidosis, a rise in acidity in the rumen, or first stomach chamber of the cow, causing the walls of the rumen to become ulcerated; and laminitis, a foot inflammation resulting in lameness.

The dairy industry results in more "downed" cows than any other kind of livestock. These sick animals often slip and fall on the way to slaughter, or are unable to walk or even stand. In the past they have been dragged with chains or carried with forklifts or front-loaders. After years of such abuses, the USDA announced a rule prohibiting the slaughter of downer cows and requiring that they instead be humanely euthanized. We can only hope there is sufficient oversight and enforcement of this law.

Male calves are of no use for dairy production. This is why we have "veal." Veal is a convenient byproduct of the dairy industry. Some calves are slaughtered at just a day or even hours old. Others – roughly two thirds of about 700,000 male calves slaughtered annually in the U.S. – are confined in small crates, with no light and barely any room to move, for about 20 weeks. They are fed a liquid milk substitute intentionally deficient in iron and fiber. When combined with their imposed lack of exercise, this diet results in anemic flesh that is then sold as "milk-fed" or "fancy" veal.

Confession: when I lived in Europe in the 1980s, one of my favorite dishes was *Wienerschnitzel*, breaded veal cutlet. It's quite easy to eat and enjoy something when we don't think about what it is or how it is produced. And I've been slower than some to understand the horrors of veal production. Veal crates have been banned in California, Arizona, Colorado, Maine, and some countries in the European Union (but not in Virginia, where I saw some on local farms on a trip through the state in fall 2016). Demand for veal has, thankfully, plummeted to an all-time low.

Eggs

I used to boast that I loved eggs and enjoyed them any way at all they could be prepared: sunny side up, over easy, scrambled, hard-boiled, soft-boiled, poached, deviled. Then I learned how eggs are produced on factory egg farms.

Egg-laying chickens are typically confined in battery cages which are so small that they have no room to spread their wings or stretch their legs. They are de-beaked, just like chickens raised for meat, to prevent aggressive behavior in close quarters.   They suffer abrasions and feather loss from rubbing their bodies against the wire walls.   The cages are stacked atop one another in massive rows inside warehouses that hold up to 100,000 birds each.   Chicken manure collects in pits under the cages, polluting the air with dust and ammonia and causing sickness.   Approximately 16 million hens among 325 million raised each year, die inside their cages.   The ones who don't are often "spent" after about one year of egg production and sent to slaughter.

California voters, to their credit, passed Proposition 2 in 2008 by a significant margin.   Proposition 2, Standards for Confining Farm Animals, resulted in, among other things, the elimination of battery cages on egg farms in California.   It requires that chickens be confined in a manner that allows them to stand up, turn around freely, and fully extend their limbs.   While this deals with only one aspect of inhumane treatment of egg-laying hens, it is at least a small step forward.

Remember the fate of male calves on dairy farms? Well, there's no equivalent of veal among chickens. Because egg-laying poultry are bred exclusively for egg production, chicks are not suitable to be profitably raised for meat.   So chicks are quickly sorted by the hundreds into male and female.   Females go on to produce eggs over the course of their brief, cruel lives.   Male chicks are often thrown into trashcans and sealed inside trash bag liners, where they suffocate or are crushed under the weight of other chicks.   Alternatively, they might be thrown into macerators (meat grinders) while they are still alive.

As if this isn't horrifying enough, there is a heart-rending scene in the documentary *Peaceable Kingdom: The Journey Home* that sheds unflattering light on how factory farm animals – chickens in particular – are regarded by corporations. (I'm not sure how the film-makers managed to capture this footage.) A tornado had struck an egg farm, destroying 12 of its 150 warehouses where chickens were housed as described above. The operators decided that, rather than relocate the thousands of chickens from the damaged barns, it was cheaper to kill them. They were scooped up with front-loaders and deposited by the hundreds into dumpsters. Each dumpster held about 10,000 chickens, so by the time they were full, one would think the chickens at the bottom were already suffocated or crushed by the weight of those above. The dumpsters were then sealed, and carbon dioxide was injected to finish the job.

To the geniuses of American capitalism, these chickens were just egg machines, not sentient living beings.

Fish and Shellfish

As we've seen from the numbers in Chapter One, what is different about fish and shellfish is that much of it is wild-caught, not farm-raised. (Remember that the numbers for both "production" categories are positively staggering.) What is the same, though, is the cruel treatment of these staggering numbers and the total disregard for living animal species other than our own. Fish, like land animals, are treated as products for our exploitation and thoughtless consumption.

Most wild-caught fish die from being crushed in nets, or from suffocation, freezing, or live dissection. These processes of death are prolonged, not quick, lasting minutes or even hours. Farm-raised fish, too, are killed by slow, inhumane methods. There are no standards for fish and shellfish equivalent to the Humane Slaughter Act (such as it is).

Finally, as we'll see later, ocean fishing entails collecting greater quantities of unwanted sea creatures in the massive fishing nets than of those species, such as cod, being harvested for human consumption. All these other animals are simply discarded, a practice that is cruel, destructive of biodiversity, and unconscionably wasteful.

So for me, the initial motivation to move away from meat, fish, dairy and eggs toward a plant-based diet was the damage from animal agriculture to global climate and the environment. With this as motivation, I might be able to feel satisfied with, say, an 80 percent cutback in my consumption of animal products. But then I learned about animal treatment, in both the meat and dairy industries. I realized that farm animals are no different from the dogs and cats we consider to be our pets. They are sentient, intelligent, loving beings. And I understood that, if I aspire to kindness and compassion as a person, my kindness and compassion should extend to all living things, not just to other humans. Who are we to think we are a superior species, entitled to exploit other animal species for our convenience, when we don't have to, when our survival by no means depends on such exploitation?

After decade upon decade of living in relative ignorance, then, I finally discovered all the ugly truths I've told you thus far about animal agriculture. I felt I had no choice but to make a commitment: I can – and will –thrive on plants.

SEVEN

Pollution

Entire books have been written on pollution from factory farming, so this chapter includes a mere sampling. This sampling, though, should suffice to alarm anyone concerned about the long-term health, stability, and quality of our environment. Certainly the greenhouse gases that are byproducts of animal agriculture – carbon dioxide, methane, and nitrous oxide – qualify as pollution. They are substances which are ultimately harmful to life and health, to put it mildly. But greenhouse gases are only a few of the pollutants resulting from factory farms. In previous chapters we've touched on some others.

Animals on factory farms generate more than 100 times the amount of excrement as the entire human population of the United States, and that excrement is not treated by sewage systems. The pollutants and toxins from animal excrement eventually make their way into groundwater and, ultimately, our oceans.

We've heard of the Great Pacific garbage patch, a huge concentration of plastic and other waste that has made its way into our oceans due to our throwaway society, wasteful use of resources, and carelessness in disposal of the tons of waste we generate daily. Well, in the Gulf of Mexico off the Louisiana coast, oxygen depletion from animal manure and fertilizer pollution, which has made its way through our waterways and down the Mississippi River, has virtually wiped out sea life –

both plant and animal – over a 7,000 square mile "dead zone." That's equivalent to a 70 by 100-mile rectangle of ocean; not only is this a huge area, but it would be foolish to think that it exists in isolation from the greater ocean area of our planet.

Let's zoom in for a moment on those hog farm "lagoons," thinly-lined ponds into which pig excrement, toxins, and occasional foreign objects are released from the massive warehouses of hog operations in North Carolina, Illinois, and Iowa. A single lagoon may measure 120,000 square feet and be up to 30 feet deep. To dispose of the contents, Smithfield borrows a practice from the old days when hog farms were small and more broadly distributed across the U.S. Journalist Jeff Tietz, in his essay "Boss Hog," describes the process succinctly: "Pollution control at Smithfield consists of spraying the pig shit from the lagoons onto the fields." Small farmers used to do this to fertilize their fields, but the volume now is so scaled up that it simply makes life miserable for anyone living near these hog operations, which, in eastern North Carolina, for example, includes a whole lot of people. These people suffer from bronchitis, diarrhea, headaches and mood disorders, even heart palpitations.

The lagoons emit methane, carbon dioxide, hydrogen sulfide, bacteria, and ammonia gas into the air. Besides air pollution, there is the problem of runoff, even though Smithfield claims that, "If you're getting runoff, you're doing something wrong."

Right. The liners of these ponds are sometimes punctured by rocks. Heavy rains and flooding – does that ever happen in North Carolina? – can cause lagoons to overflow. Pig shit – sorry, excrement – has been shown to raise the level of nitrogen and phosphorus in receiving rivers by as much as six times. In North Carolina, the Cape Fear and Neuse River basins are affected by most of the hog operations in the state.

A record spill occurred in 1995 when the dike of a 120,000-square-foot lagoon ruptured, releasing its contents into the headwaters of the New River. (In fairness to Smithfield, the lagoon belonged to one of their competitors.) Over two months the spill made its way to the ocean. More than 1 million fish died.

Then there are hurricanes. Hurricane Floyd in 1999 put many North Carolina lagoons underwater. A brown flow from a half dozen waterways converged in Albemarle-Pamlico Sound and flowed from there into the Atlantic, wiping out most freshwater marine life along the way. Again in 2016, Hurricane Matthew caused flooding of fourteen lagoons, polluting groundwater used for drinking. As the Spanish philosopher Santayana wrote long ago, "Those who cannot remember the past are condemned to repeat it."

Hurricanes will, of course, become more common as a cumulative effect of continuing climate change.

North Carolina has passed a moratorium on new hog operations, but 4,000 lagoons built before 1997 are still in use, and hog farming in North Carolina and elsewhere will continue full throttle until consumers decide that enough is enough.

EIGHT

Labor

We've seen, in disturbing detail, some of the living conditions and abusive treatment of factory farm animals – cows, pigs, chickens, and turkeys.   Although the industry does its best to conceal its business practices from scrutiny, animal rights groups have managed over the years to expose some aspects of meat, dairy, and egg production to the public eye.   As people learn more about how farm animals are treated, they are, for the most part, repelled by what they see.

But there is yet another species that is poorly treated by the corporations engaged in animal agriculture: humans.   The workers in factory farm facilities perform hazardous jobs (made even more hazardous by the speed of production).   They are poorly paid, work long hours, and suffer from job-related accidents, repetitive motion injuries, respiratory problems, and post-traumatic stress disorder.

We've already seen the job of the "stunner" in beef production: firing 7-inch bolts into the foreheads of cattle hour after hour, day after day.   We can surmise that the ergonomics of performing this task might lead to strained backs and repetitive motion injuries.

Journalist Christopher D. Cook, in his essay "Sliced and Diced: The Labor You Eat," writes, "Even speedier than the slaughtered pig or cow, the dead chicken may be the fastest animal in North America."   Chicken production includes the following enticing job titles:

catcher, hanger, evisc (evisceration) and debone. "Catchers" select chickens for slaughter inside holding pens where temperatures can approach 100 degrees and the air reeks of ammonia and fecal matter. These workers are subjected to constant urination by terrified chickens. Cuts, eye infections, and respiratory ailments are common among catchers. "Hangers" attach the feet of birds into metal shackles (just up the line from slaughter) at line speeds of up to 50 birds a minute. Rotator cuff injuries are widespread.

Farther down the line from the automated slaughter, and beyond the scalding tanks that facilitate rapid plucking of the feathers, workers in "evisc" pull and twist the innards from 35 or more chickens a minute. Farther on still, boneless chicken breasts (the chicken part in highest demand by consumers) are created in "debone" by workers who chop and slice through joints, tendons, and gristle. It's not unusual for these workers to cut themselves or their neighbors when the blades of their scissors or knives slip. Many workers in evisc and debone suffer repetitive stress disorders as well.

And remember bioethicist Peter Singer's graphic description of how turkeys are inseminated (since their oversized breasts render them incapable of mating)? I wonder what the job title is of the workers who masturbate the male turkeys.

What recourse do factory farm workers have against these kinds of working conditions, as well as the low pay, long hours, and lack of benefits? Not much.

The animal agriculture industry employs mostly economically desperate, undocumented workers; white workers generally won't take these jobs. The immigrant workers who do take them bring with them the lowest of expectations; they are used to receiving low pay for hard work. Most factory farm jobs are non-union jobs paying $6-9 per hour or, hopefully, minimum wage in states where the minimum wage is higher. Factory farm wages have actually fallen since 1980; this is a trend that echoes other sectors of corporate America, but worse because these workers' wages were so low to start with. As a result, few factory farm workers have health insurance; they can't afford it. Turnover is high, and the industry likes it this way, because it makes it more difficult for workers to organize.

The pressure for production speed – in order to increase profit margins –makes these jobs all the more hazardous and injury-prone. During the Reagan administration the poultry industry successfully lobbied the Department of Agriculture to allow an increase in line speeds from 70 to 91 birds per minute. And it wasn't until 1998 that the United Food and Commercial Workers (UFCW), representing factory farm workers, won their right to bathroom breaks. Prior to that, poultry and meatpacking workers were often forced to relieve themselves at their workstations. Sadly, as Christopher Cook states in his essay, "food processing workers and unions are battling relentlessly for things that ought to be taken for granted."

As a nation, we're beginning to understand that plenty of corporations in plenty of industries – construction, landscaping, clothing, fast food, and others – are quite happy to employ and exploit undocumented workers. It's great for their bottom line. So animal agriculture is not unique, just one of the worst.

NINE

Health

This chapter will focus on human health, as opposed to the health of farm animals. The numerous risks to human health from the industry practices described in preceding chapters are fairly obvious, so I won't repeat them all here. Rather I'd like to focus on the health effects of the food we eat and a few of the contrasts between meat consumption and a plant-based diet. This chapter is by no means a comprehensive discussion of healthy diet. Diet is a complex subject, and science is learning more about it all the time, which often results in changing dietary guidelines and some confusion among consumers.

With Howard Lyman as my guide, let me discuss just a few of the adverse effects of meat consumption. Besides subjecting himself to the health risks of working with fertilizers and chemicals as a cattle rancher (which probably caused the spinal tumor that almost paralyzed him), Lyman was a poster child for eating meat. He writes in his wonderful book, *Mad Cowboy: Plain Truth from the Cattle Rancher Who Won't Eat Meat*, that he was more than 130 pounds overweight, his cholesterol was over 300, and his blood pressure was dangerously high. He jokes that when he first decided to stop eating meat, he went through a stage where he became the world's worst vegetarian, consuming great quantities of eggs, cheese, bread, sugar, and other carbohydrates. Eventually, though, he took the extra step and became vegan, eliminating dairy and eggs. He lost 130 pounds, his cholesterol fell to 140, and his blood pressure dropped into normal range.

Although vegans might need to consume a greater volume of food than those who eat meat, they will tend to lose weight naturally and be healthier, because they are eating foods that are much lower in saturated fat. Saturated fat makes up a large share of animal fat.

Lyman very honestly points out that it is possible even for vegans to be overweight, by using too much vegetable oil; eating great quantities of bread, pasta, French fries, and potato chips; or even consuming too much peanut butter or eating too many olives and avocados. (I fear I'm sometimes guilty of this, but I compensate with a fairly active lifestyle, exercise, and a naturally high metabolism.)

According to Dr. Neal Barnard, a plant-based diet should come from four "new" food groups: fruit, vegetables, whole grains, and legumes (beans, peas, lentils). Thankfully, for me, these groups make possible a plethora of "meat analogues" (substitutes), most of which are high-protein and do a great job replicating – or improving upon – the taste and texture of meat.

In making the transition from meat and dairy products to a plant-based diet, three important nutrients to pay close attention to are protein, calcium, and vitamin B12. Calcium is easy. You will no longer get calcium from milk, but leafy green vegetables are loaded with it. In increasing order, romaine lettuce, kale, collard greens (my personal favorite), turnip greens, and bok choy all contain more calcium than milk on a per-calorie basis.

Protein is pretty easy, too. If you take the path of replacing meat with meat analogues, you can get much of the daily protein you need in that way alone. In addition, although you'll no longer be getting protein from milk, cheese, and eggs, instead you'll find plenty in nuts, grains, and tofu.

Vitamin B12 is a bit trickier. You don't need much B12, and your body is good at storing it. Vitamin B12 is found neither in animals nor plants; rather it grows on bacteria and fungi. People who eat meat get B12 because animals eat dirt and manure along with their feed. Isn't that a cheery thought? So, on a plant-based diet you could get your B12 by not washing your vegetables – not recommended. The better answer is supplements. Multivitamins like Centrum contain all the B12 you need; just add them to your daily routine if you haven't already.

One other important health risk from meat goes away if we all eat plants instead, and factory farms go the way of the dinosaur. Most of the antibiotics sold in the United States today are routinely fed to livestock, because of the high risk of disease from close confinement as well as other unhealthful industry practices. Administering all these antibiotics to animals brings with it the risk that "superbug" organisms will evolve which are resistant to them. This, in turn, means that these antibiotics are no longer effective in treating humans. European Union countries manage this potential risk to humans by administering antibiotics only to animals that are sick.

Let me end this chapter on a positive note. The following diseases are rampant in the United States and are among our leading causes of death:

- Type 2 diabetes
- Cardiovascular disease
- Hypertension (high blood pressure)

- Stroke
- Obesity
- Prostate cancer
- Colon cancer

A plant-based diet can reduce the risk of mortality from *all* of these ailments. So, on a plant-based diet, you will find that you can not only *survive* – but *thrive*!

TEN

Sustainability

As global population keeps increasing and as the power of large corporations has grown to unhealthy levels, we see the U.S. and other economies engaging in more and more business practices that are *unsustainable.* What does this mean – unsustainable? It means doing something that cannot continue indefinitely, something that, due to finite resources, or due to external limitations or negative consequences of some sort, will eventually cease of its own weight. The wise action in the case of such practices would be to voluntarily cease or at least curtail unsustainable behavior, and thereby avoid or at least limit damage. Yet the momentum of capitalism, somehow, always seems to favor continuing unsustainable business practices, as long as they are profitable in the near term. The fossil fuel industry has become the poster child for unsustainable business practices; animal agriculture is right behind it.

We've seen many examples in previous chapters of environmental damage and resource depletion from animal agriculture that make the industry unsustainable. Let's just consolidate them here to remind ourselves. It will help us comprehend the scope and magnitude of the threats posed by factory farming to human well-being and to the health of the planet.

Today it is already impossible to feed the world's population at American levels of meat and dairy consumption. Recently developed countries like China seem to be emulating American behavior by eating more meat as their people become more prosperous; if this trend continues, it will only exacerbate world hunger and starvation. There is, on the other hand, the theoretical possibility of feeding the entire global population a plant-based diet, with even some room for growth.

We cannot continue to produce meat and dairy products at current levels of land and water use. For one thing, water – especially clean water – is increasingly scarce and needed for greater purposes, like sustaining life. 660 gallons of water to produce a hamburger is outrageously unsustainable. The Ogallala Aquifer is dropping at a frightening rate. And as we've seen, using so much land for livestock grazing in the U.S. is crowding out other animal species like horses. Clearing the Amazon rainforest to raise cattle cannot continue for long; its impact on global carbon dioxide levels is accelerating catastrophic climate change. And lastly, animal agriculture is degrading land and water quality through over-grazing and through animal waste products and toxins bleeding into our waterways and groundwater supply.

I spared you a lengthy discussion of fish in the chapter on animal treatment. But we can't ignore the oceans and the sea life they contain. Depletion of fish populations has many causes; notable among them are overfishing and wasteful fishing practices. Industrialized fishing today is done primarily with massive nets. For every pound of fish caught for food, such as "wild-caught" cod, there is up to five pounds of untargeted species caught: dolphins, whales, sea turtles, etc. This is called "bycatch" or "bykill," and is simply discarded as the cost of doing business.

And guess what farmed fish are fed? Wild fish.

In addition, degradation of sea life and species destruction from pollution, global warming, and methane release are leading to a future where *all fish* may be gone as early as the year 2048. Don't think that this will be destructive only to oceans and sea life; there will be heavy collateral damage to land-based life as well. Earth is an *ecosystem*, where all forms of life, land and sea, plant and animal, are interrelated.

None of this is sustainable. Yet overshadowing everything else are the devastating effects of rising levels of greenhouse gases in our atmosphere: carbon dioxide, methane, and nitrous oxide. If we don't act soon, on both fossil fuel and animal product consumption, climate change will bring an end to countless other species, possibly including *homo sapiens*, sooner than we think. "Unsustainable" grossly understates the magnitude of the crisis we're creating through our own actions.

ELEVEN

What to Eat?

At last it's time to look ahead at where we're going, instead of dwelling further on all the negatives of where we are and what we need to be running away from. This chapter is all good news.

What this chapter is *not*, though, is a comprehensive guide on how to go vegan and maintain a perfectly balanced diet. Many books are available to help you here, written by dieticians and nutrition specialists who are far more qualified than I to talk about such things. In addition, there are dozens of vegan cookbooks, if you are one who enjoys cooking.

Rather, what I want to do here is provide the encouragement to get you started. And let me be honest. When I first started shopping for and trying vegan products, I encountered what I would politely call some nasty stuff – food I just *did not like*. That said, though, our taste in food is highly personal; something I dislike might strike you as fine, or vice versa. The point is that I'm now in a place, after about a year of vegan lifestyle, where I have an immense variety of delectable food items to replace the meat, fish, dairy, and eggs, that I used to like – or thought I did. Now that I've reached this place, I can honestly tell you that adopting a vegan diet *is not a sacrifice*. I enjoy food as much as or more than I ever did, and at the same time I have the satisfaction of knowing that now I'm a better global citizen. An important purpose of this book is to give you a head start getting to your own better place.

So first let me talk in some generalities. There are a hundred ways to eat vegan, depending on your personal preferences. Today, compared to only a few years ago, there are more and more vegan items on the market, widely available. Although the best sources for vegan items are usually smaller regional markets such as Trader Joe's, Mother's Market, Whole Foods, Sprouts, etc., most large supermarket chains offer some vegan items as well: Ralphs/Kroger, Vons/Safeway, Wegmans, Stater Bros. (in Southern California), etc. Finally, I'm a fan of farmers' markets and buying locally from small businesspeople, where producer and consumer live in close proximity. This is good for capitalism as well as for climate. After all, why should we be dependent upon products of huge corporations that must be shipped hundreds or thousands of miles to reach us?

Many restaurants offer vegan, or at least vegetarian, items on their menus. Often you can find vegan/vegetarian options on menus of Italian, Mexican, Indian, Japanese, and Vietnamese restaurants. Many restaurants will adapt their entrees upon request, so don't be afraid to ask. Menus of many Thai restaurants commonly offer a choice with each entrée: beef, chicken, shrimp, pork, or fried tofu (choose tofu, the vegan option). Even fast food chains have begun adapting to the vegan/vegetarian market. Subway offers a "local favorite" veggie patty sub, quite satisfying, and you can customize your sandwich with all vegan ingredients. Del Taco, a Southern California Mexican food chain, has an eight-layer veggie burrito, which I love. Upon request, they can hold the cheese and sour cream. Personally, I was never a fan of Burger King, but now that they offer a veggie burger in their restaurants all over the U.S., I've become an occasional customer when traveling (ask them to hold the mayo).

More recently, Red Robin, the national gourmet burger chain, has added both a veggie burger and vegan burger option to their full menu at most of their locations; any of their burgers can be customized to suit either a vegetarian or vegan diet. I applaud Red Robin for taking this important step.

Memo to McDonald's: With your mammoth share of the fast food market, isn't it time to add some vegan breakfast and dinner choices to your continually evolving menu?

Best of all, entirely vegan restaurants are popping up all over the country. There is an Android app, Happy Cow, that can help you locate vegan or vegetarian food in your area.

Here's a side note: I live in California, but I have roots in upstate New York and travel across country and in the eastern U.S. on occasion. Based on this limited experience, I believe that, if you live in California as I do, your transition to a plant-based diet might be even easier than in many other parts of the country. California leads in many things, because of its great diversity and progressivism; the trend away from meat and dairy consumption is no exception.

Let me caution you again that, although there are a hundred ways to eat vegan, this chapter will be biased somewhat by my personal preferences and individual tastes. I'll try at least to be up front about this, but please be aware that many other options are open to you.

First, you'll be happy to know, as I was, that you don't have to change everything. I'm fortunate to have always liked vegetables, fruits, nuts, cereals, and grains, and you can keep on eating these. Nuts, beans, and grains are good sources of protein, to replace the protein you no longer get from consuming meat and other animal products. If I feel the need for a quick dose of protein on a given day, I find cashews easily meet that need. Many (not all) cereals and breads are vegan without being explicitly labeled as such; read the ingredients to see if they are free of dairy and eggs.

I used to like meat – or at least I thought I did. Now, having since discovered a vast array of meat analogues and with the advantage of hindsight, I realize that it was probably never the meat itself I liked, but rather how it was flavored and textured. The taste of animal fat is now repulsive to me, and probably it was always how that taste was obscured with salt, pepper, spices, and sauces that made meat enjoyable for me in the first place. That said, I wouldn't be where I am right now without meat analogues. Some vegans have no use for them and are content with vegetables, grains, beans, etc. I don't know if I'll ever become that kind of vegan. Are meat analogues merely necessary to help me through some sort of transition to vegan perfection? Not really. Meat analogues are fine, because they are entirely plant-based and often comparable in protein content to the animal products they replace.

And most of all, vegan meat analogues are pleasing to my palate. Chicken and turkey analogues are particularly good, and their texture is perfect. Beef, fish, even pork analogues are a close second to the poultry.

Here I'll mention two brands that provide me with all the meat analogues I'll ever need. Gardein is a national brand with a wide selection of products; let me simply say that I haven't tried a Gardein product yet that I don't like. Gardein products usually come frozen, in foil pouches, and can be easily and quickly microwaved, pan-fried, or baked in a conventional oven. They are rich in protein.

Even better, last year at a farmers' market in Southern California I met Kerry Song, a young entrepreneur who is building a small business selling plant-based meats with all natural ingredients. The name of her company is The Abbot's Butcher. She also sells online at **theabbotsbutcher.com** and is working hard to enter the retail grocery market. Among her product offerings are "beef" burgers, Italian "meatballs," Spanish "chorizo," and ground "chicken." I can attest that these products are high quality; they replicate or improve upon the taste and texture of meat (without the fatty under-taste); they are very high in protein; and they can be prepared in the same manner as the animal products they replace. The Abbot's Butcher works particularly well for me, not just for all of these reasons, but because I prefer to support local businesses whenever possible. (It helps, too, that Kerry is so pleasant to deal with.)

To be completely honest, I still like the taste of cheese. Fortunately, though, I no longer "need" it. Although it took some trial and error, I've found vegan versions of cheddar and mozzarella – shredded, sliced, and in block form – that taste just as good and have the same texture as real cheese. Daiya and Field Roast have some excellent vegan "cheeses;" I'm sure there are other brands as well. So now I can still enjoy a cheeseburger, pizza, or cheese and crackers without the guilt from knowing that a dairy cow was mistreated to make them possible.

There are excellent vegan butters that taste, spread, and melt just like dairy butter. I use a soy-free product from Earth Balance (they offer other variations as well), and I've been told that Miyoko butter substitute is also very good.

As I mentioned earlier, I absolutely used to love eggs. And while I always knew that an animal had been killed in order for me to eat meat (but, from old habits and training, never gave it too much thought), I had no idea at all how much cruelty was involved in putting that egg on my plate. No more. My own solution now is possible thanks to an ingenious product called The Vegg. It's a powder that, when mixed with water, perfectly duplicates the taste of egg yolk. It can be used to make French toast or combined with tofu to make a tofu scramble or a fried egg sandwich. For a really special treat, I add Spanish "chorizo" from The Abbot's Butcher to my tofu scramble.

A word of caution is in order here. Some vegan products, although they replicate the flavor and texture of the animal products they replace, are by no means nutritionally equivalent. The Vegg is one of these; it has almost no food value, but the flavor is perfect. This means only that I need to eat other things as well in order to maintain a nutritionally balanced diet.

As an adult I've used milk primarily to pour on cold cereal. The health benefits of real cow's milk are highly overrated, even somewhat controversial. Besides, there are many plant-based milks to choose from: almond milk, soy milk, coconut milk, etc., either plain or flavored. My personal preference is organic plain soy milk from WestSoy, available at my local Trader Joe's market.

For coffee drinkers who shun black coffee, there are excellent soy creamers available. I used soy creamer at first, but I've since come to prefer my coffee black. And yes, thankfully, coffee is vegan! But do look for fair trade and organic brands.

Some of my vegan friends would probably consider me a junk food vegan. I don't mind admitting to this. My policy is, and always has been, that the healthy approach to life is to indulge in all things in moderation. Gene Baur of Farm Sanctuary likes to joke that French fries, Oreo cookies and most potato chips are vegan – and in fact they are. And here's more good news: most chocolate with greater than 70 percent cocoa is also vegan. Delicious vegan ice creams (frozen non-dairy desserts) abound. Although somewhat harder to find, there are even some excellent vegan donuts.

Here are just some of the brands that offer vegan products, listed alphabetically: The Abbot's Butcher, Amy's, Beyond Meat, Daiya, Earth Balance, Field Roast, Follow Your Heart, Full Circle, Gardein, Hampton Creek, Lightlife, Miyoko, Sweet Earth, Trader Joe's, Yves. There are three important things to note about these brands and the companies that market products under them:

- The list is by no means comprehensive, but all of these brands – and more – comprise part of my vegan diet.

- I have no financial or business interest in any of these brands or companies; I'm simply a consumer.
- Some of these brands also offer products containing meat, dairy, and eggs, so please look for the vegan "V" symbol on the package and read the ingredients carefully the first time you consider a given item.

There's a whole new world out there – healthy, satisfying, and compassionate. I encourage you to have fun exploring. If you encounter something that doesn't appeal to you, just keep looking for equivalent items; I can almost guarantee you'll find something that works.

TWELVE

A Better World

Circling back to the overarching issue for our planet, climate change, I honestly don't know – no one does – if humanity will ultimately survive the fossil fuel era. We might have already passed the tipping point, where feedback loops among our atmosphere and land and oceans will soon be unleashed. The power of the fossil fuel industry is formidable, and it will take time, at best – time we might not have – to convert the global economy to 100 percent renewable energy. The carbon dioxide already in our atmosphere will take a hundred years or more to dissipate.

Our days on this planet may be numbered, but perhaps, rather than just give up and brace for the inevitable, we should do all we can to extend our existence as long as possible, and make it as livable as possible. Although it's become practically a cliché among climate activists, don't we care about the futures of our children and grandchildren?

Right now – today – our lives are still tolerable. This is not necessarily true for everyone; the poor around the globe are already suffering the effects of climate change and environmental destruction. But for some of us, at least, life is still tolerable, even quite comfortable. We are all in this together. If we take bold action now against climate change, not only we, but others already suffering, will benefit. If we do nothing, not only others, but we, will suffer.

So certainly we should keep pressuring government and industry for a transformation from fossil fuels to renewable energy. But we have seen now that there is another significant industrial sector contributing to climate change: animal agriculture. This industry, too, is powerful and resistant to change, but there is one key difference. As individuals, we are not enslaved by animal products, as we are by fossil fuels (at least in the short term). In the case of animal products, the alternative is readily available to us: plants. Each of us as individuals could make the choice today, or tomorrow, or next week or next month to stop eating animal products. There is nothing the industry could do to stop us.

In changing our diet from animal products to plants, we might at least prolong our life on this planet. Remember, methane, 86 times more potent as a greenhouse gas than carbon dioxide, persists in the atmosphere for only about 25 years. Nitrous oxide, even more potent, is also short-lived. A change we could all make now – at least in theory – will pay off within the lifetimes of many of us.

But there's more. My own journey to this place began with an awakening to the climate and environmental effects of animal agriculture. Then, along the way I learned also about the inhumane treatment of the animals we feel entitled to exploit for food. So whether or not we can prevail against catastrophic climate change, however long humanity has left on this planet, it seems to me that in the meantime the world would be better with more compassion. More compassion for fellow humans, to be sure, but perhaps if we enlarge our concept of compassion to include other animal species beyond our own, we would find it easier to have greater compassion for our fellow man as well.

And while we're speaking of compassion, there is another aspect of "vegan" that goes beyond food and diet. "Vegan" is a type of diet – yes – but it is also a philosophy, a lifestyle, centered on compassion for all. The vegan philosophy encompasses concern for exploitation of animal species in any manner. This includes leather products, fashion furs, clothing and cosmetics and other consumer products made using animal ingredients. As with food, there are perfectly good alternatives. Although it might be inconvenient, at first, to eliminate all such products, it is a goal worth working toward. We don't need to buy products made with animal ingredients.

I've given some thought lately to how the demise of animal agriculture would play out. What would happen to those 70 billion farm animals that are slaughtered each year? Well, in my view, as demand for meat and dairy falls, the industry would cease breeding billions of animals for which there is no longer a demand. Depending on how precipitous the drop in demand is, there would probably be some abandonment, suffering, slaughter, or die-off of farm animals already born, or soon to be born. There is probably no way to avoid this. But for the most part, farm animal population would diminish due to animals no longer born and bred. In this sense, the end of animal agriculture would entail far less suffering and carnage than its continuation.

Howard Lyman, with his typical bluntness, presents us with a fundamental choice: "The question we must ask ourselves as a culture," he writes, "is whether we want to embrace the change that must come, or resist it." For me, the possibility of a more sustainable, less violent world, even as we enter an era of global crisis, will at least make the world better while we still have it.

ACKNOWLEDGMENTS

No book worth the paper it's printed on (or the Kindle storage it occupies) is a solo effort, and this one is no exception. This book is a collaboration and, for me, one of the most rewarding aspects of writing it has been the support and friendship of those who participated in its production. I get to put my name on the cover, but without the efforts of these people, there would be no book.

Barbara English, perhaps without realizing it, planted the seed in my brain for the idea that a book such as this was needed. I also blame her entirely for my becoming vegan – at least the best vegan I know how to be so far. Once I finished the manuscript, Barbara reviewed it with the utmost attention to detail. She put her heart and soul into the process. Besides suggesting minor improvements to content and accuracy, she identified several important ideas I had omitted; I have since incorporated them. Beyond any doubt, she made the end product better.

Matt Ball of Farm Sanctuary also reviewed the manuscript with a critical eye, advising improvements and providing a valuable fact-check. I deeply appreciate his willingness to contribute his valuable time. To repay him, I've done my best to make a strong case for saving the chickens.

My heartfelt thanks to Kerry Song, owner of The Abbot's Butcher, for believing in the book from the start and for all her encouragement along the way. Kerry, too, offered suggestions that made the finished product better.

And thanks, Kerry, for all the delectable, easy-to-prepare recipes using your natural, plant-based products; you'll make a cook out of me yet.

Finally, the cover of a book might be its most critical feature. Without an attractive, enticing cover that captures potential readers' attention, a book may have no readers at all. Graphic design and art are not my strengths, but luckily I know someone whose strengths they are. My friend and fellow vegan Rachael Steinke generously contributed her time and talent to create a cover we can both be proud of.

RECOMMENDED READING AND

VIEWING

In keeping with my purpose in writing this book – to provide a concise and convincing account of my journey to a plant-based diet – I'll mention just a few of the many excellent documentaries and books that guided me. These are the works that made the greatest impact upon my thinking. I hope they will prove as meaningful and engaging for you.

Documentaries

Cowspiracy: The Sustainability Secret is the film that first opened my eyes to the negative consequences of animal agriculture. While it focuses heavily on climate and environmental issues, it also touches very gently on animal treatment. I've lost count of the number of friends who have watched it since I first did and been moved to take action. It is now available for streaming on Netflix. You can also download the film or purchase the DVD on-line at **www.cowspiracy.com**.

Peaceable Kingdom: The Journey Home features several farmers, including Howard Lyman, who have abandoned raising animals for food. It is a powerful treatise on the cruelty of animal agriculture and a hopeful look at an alternative scenario of compassion. You can watch it free on-line at **www.tribeofheart.org**.

Forks Over Knives goes into depth on human health issues, drawing sharp contrasts between eating meat versus plants. You can purchase the DVD or download the film at **www.forksoverknives.com/the-film/**.

Books

Three books in particular have been invaluable to me in making my own transition to a plant-based diet, and also as resources for writing this book.

The Sustainability Secret: Rethinking Our Diet to Transform the World, by Kip Andersen and Keegan Kuhn, is the book version of the *Cowspiracy* documentary. The book was published subsequent to the release of the film and covers all of the issues in the film in even greater detail.

Mad Cowboy: Plain Truth from the Cattle Rancher Who Won't Eat Meat, by Howard F. Lyman, is Lyman's personal story, from cattle rancher to politician to activist, as well as a thoroughly compelling argument for a plant-based diet.

The CAFO Reader: The Tragedy of Industrial Animal Factories, edited by Daniel Imhoff, is a compendium of essays by journalists and experts covering all aspects of Concentrated Animal Feeding Operations (CAFOs).

Another excellent book, *Comfortably Unaware: What We Choose to Eat Is Killing Us and Our Planet*, by Dr. Richard A. Oppenlander, offers a highly readable, concise discussion of the impacts of the food we eat on climate and the environment.

WELL-KNOWN VEGANS

Here is a short list of well-known personalities who are vegan, or at least close to it. It goes without saying that the world is far from perfect, but these individuals, motivated by health or environment or animal treatment or any of the multitude of reasons discussed in this book, have moved significantly toward thriving on a plant-based diet. Besides the names below, there are many more.

POLITICS
   Senator Corey Booker
   Al Gore
   Arnold Schwarzenegger

MEDIA / JOURNALISM / LAW / SCIENCE
   Lisa Bloom
   Brian Greene
   Chris Hedges and Eunice Wong
   Jane Velez-Mitchell

ENTERTAINMENT
   Casey Affleck
   Alec Baldwin
   Russell Brand
   Brendan Brazier
   James and Susie Cameron
   James Cromwell
   Ellen DeGeneres
   Peter Dinklage
   Woody Harrelson

Liam Hemsworth
Paul McCartney
Moby
Alanis Morissette
Kevin Nealon
Joaquin Phoenix
Natalie Portman
Alicia Silverstone
Loretta Swit
Carrie Underwood
Usher
Kat Von D

SPORTS
David Carter
Carl Lewis
Venus and Serena Williams